QUICK
Affirmations
FOR SUPER BUSY
WOMEN

A TO Z OF EASY PICK-ME-UPS
FOR NOT-SO-EASY DAYS

Written by
Kim Ann and **Yobe Qiu**

Illustrated by
Nejla Shojaie

This book belongs to:

_____

To our daughters,

Kayla and Jean.

Your thoughts and words can make a difference. Success will always be yours if you think and believe with your heart, mind, and soul.

Remember, anything is possible.

xoxo Mom

Welcome!

Need a little pick-me-up? We're so glad you're here!

This is your first step toward a brighter, happier future!

When life's challenges begin to feel overwhelming, it's essential to take time out to reflect and recenter. Leave negativity in the past where it belongs and focus on positive affirmations that remind you of all the good in your life.

We are two women who know what it's like never to have enough hours in a day and know some days are not-so-easy. When it rains, it pours. But - we understand how important it is to develop a strong, positive growth mindset.

Regularly reading and reciting positive affirmations can help you build confidence and resilience, as it did for us! You can develop a growth mindset that enables you to be the very best version of yourself.

That's why we created this book, an A-to-Z affirmation collection, to help you boost your mood and transform your mindset.

On the pages of this book, you'll find affirmations designed for busy women just like you. Read them, believe them, and begin to embrace a life of happiness, positivity, and abundance.

We can't wait to help you grow.

Happy reading!

Kim & Yobe

I *Appreciate* MYSELF AND *Acknowledge* MY STRENGTHS.

I AM *Bold* AND *Brilliant.*

I AM
Deserving
AND
I AM
Determined.

I

MYSELF AND OTHERS ALONG THE WAY.

I AM
Forgiving
OF MYSELF.
I WILL
BE FINE.

I AM

Grateful

FOR MY
FAMILY,
MY BUSINESS,
MY GROWTH.

I AM Good.

I
AM *Honorable*
AND
DESERVE
Happiness.

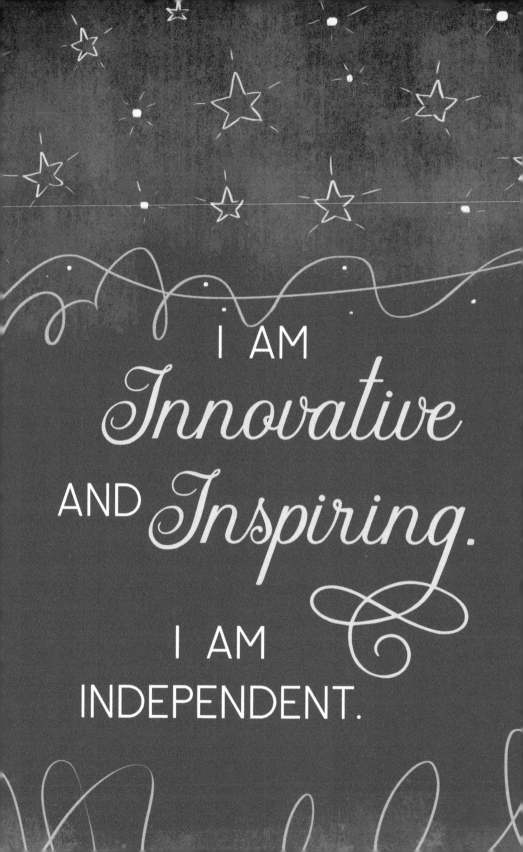

I AM *Kind*
TO MYSELF
AND KIND
TO OTHERS.

I AM *Loving* AND *Loyal.*

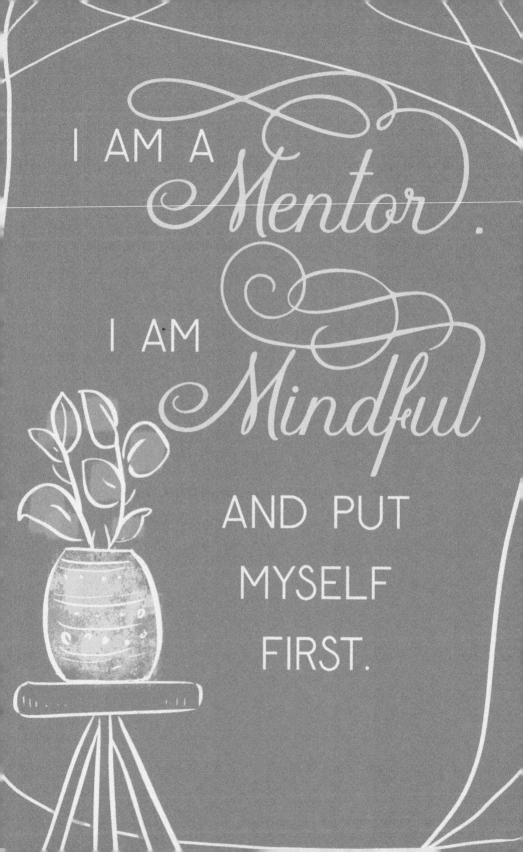

I AM A *Mentor*.

I AM *Mindful*

AND PUT MYSELF FIRST.

I AM
Needed

AND *Noble.*

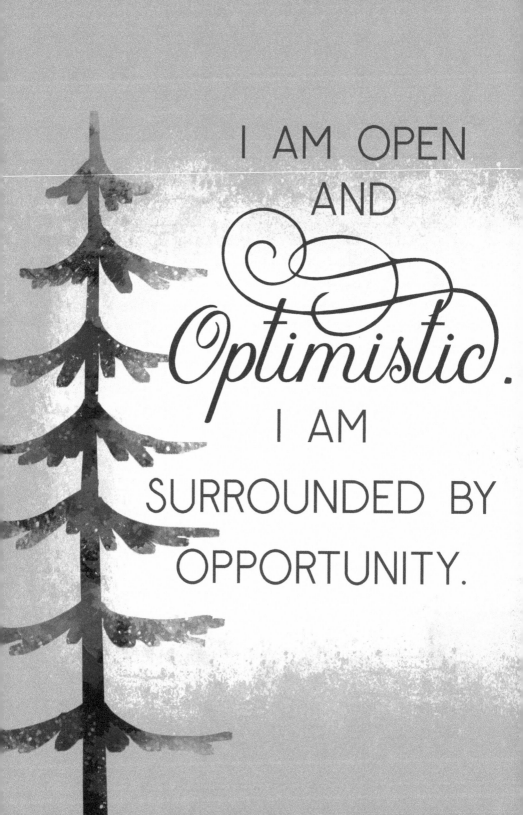

I AM OPEN AND *Optimistic.* I AM SURROUNDED BY OPPORTUNITY.

I AM

Passionate

AND

Productive.

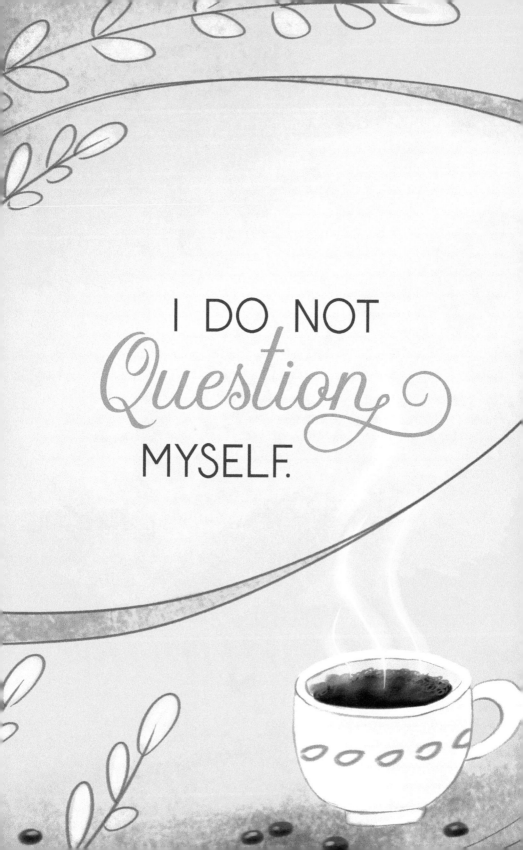

I DO NOT
Question
MYSELF.

I AM
Resourceful
AND
Reliable.

I AM
SUCCESSFUL
AND SUPPORTED.

I AM *Satisfied.*

I VALUE
MY TIME.

I AM *Tough,*

TRUSTWORTHY,
AND
THOUGHTFUL.

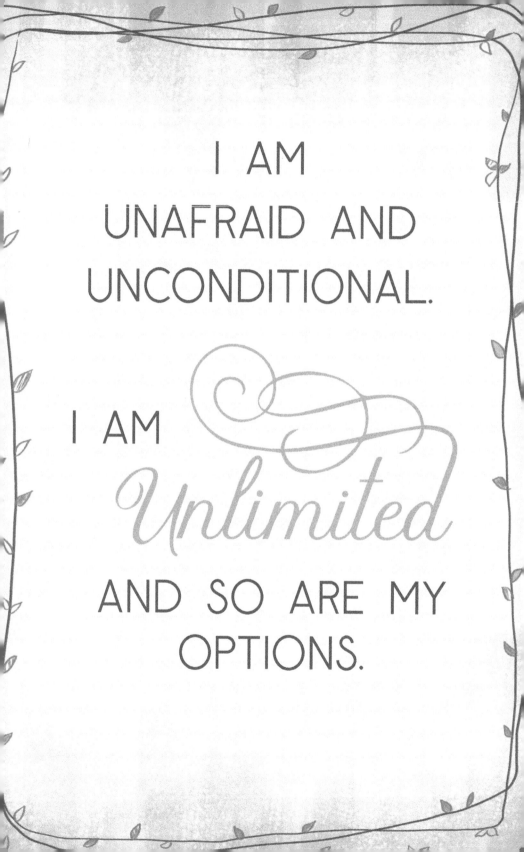

I AM
UNAFRAID AND
UNCONDITIONAL.

I AM
Unlimited
AND SO ARE MY
OPTIONS.

I HAVE GREAT

Vision

FOR
WHERE I
WANT TO BE.

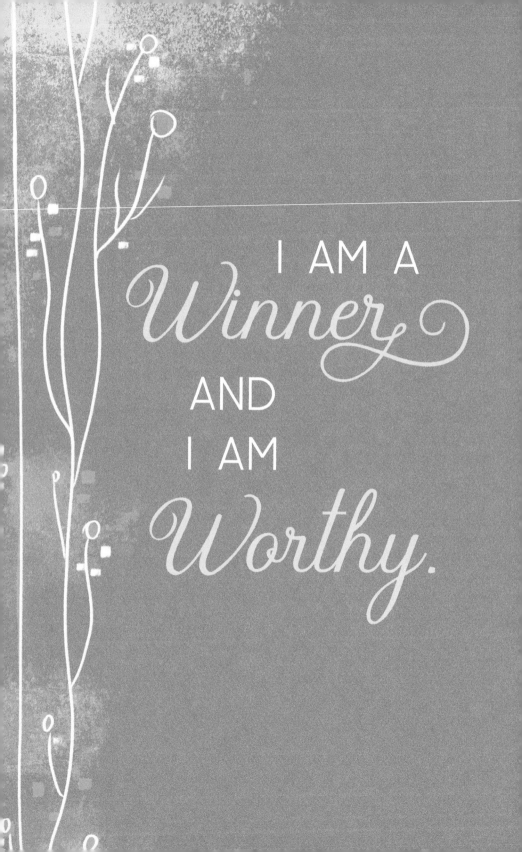

I AM A

Winner

AND

I AM

Worthy.

I AM

Xenacious.

I EMBRACE
CHANGE!

I SAY

"Yes,"

TO THE THINGS
I WANT.

I AM *Zen*
AND I AM AT PEACE!

Affirmations

_____

_____

_____

_____

_____

_____

_____

_____

_____

_____

_____

_____

_____

_____

_____

_____

_____

_____

Affirmations

Affirmations

CPSIA information can be obtained
at www.ICGtesting.com
Printed in the USA
LVHW072003030322
712272LV00004B/6